CRY FOR THE CHILDREN

DONNA DEAL

AUTHOR

Printed in the United States of America

ISBN 979-8-89114-282-4 (sc)
ISBN 979-8-89114-283-1 (e)

Library of Congress Control Number: 2026906878

2026.04.06

MainSpring Books
5901 W. Century Blvd
Suite 750
Los Angeles, CA, US, 90045

www.mainspringbooks.com

Contents

1

A Rough Life

My father and mother were divorced right after we moved back to California from Hawaii, leaving my mother with the difficult task of being on her own with not even a 10th grade education and no work experience trying to raise us at ages 5 years old, 3 years old, and 18 months. I remember the "good" experiences about living in Hawaii and I think it was because we were all together as a family in those days and the last time I recall seeing my father, as a very little child, until years later.

Life was rough for us kids because we only had our mother to rely upon. Dad had remarried and adopted his new wife's three kids and had a child by her. He stopped paying child support of one hundred fifty dollars a month for his own three kids. Mom was the youngest of seven children, none of which finished school. In the tenth grade the teacher said something to her she didn't like so she hurled her book at the teacher which resulted in the end of her high school days.

This limited education made it very difficult for her to find a decent paying job.

Our very hot temper mother was a beautiful woman and had the ability to get help from men without trying too hard. One such man, a business tycoon she met in a bar, offered her a job as a hostess at this upscale bar near D.C. assuring her it was good money. The job required her to work at night. This meant that she would have to find someone to take care of us since we were still very young.

2

Living on the Farm

As time went on, Mom found herself unable to work and care for three small children so she was faced with the decision to find us a home where the three of us would be able to stay together, so she moved us from northern, VA to a farm in Mt. Jackson, VA. with people we would end up calling Aunt Ester and Uncle George. Of course, Mom also had distant relatives close by who were Uncle Rob and Great Aunt Mary, making it easy for us to bounce back and forth for visits. One morning on a visit to their house, one armed Uncle Rob gathered up all the kittens on the farm and put them in the front yard. My sister, Keri, was playing with them, thinking how nice it was for Uncle Rob to bring them to her. Next, he went into the house and came out holding his rifle and a bucket. My sister and I were terrified watching and wondering what he was going to do. In just a few seconds he proceeded to shoot each one of them and gathered their little bodies up and put them in the bucket. My sister had nightmares for a long time after the incident.

3

Oh No, Not the Beans!

Many years later, after the kitten incident, I learned that Uncle Rob use to go out drinking with the boys and would come home drunk and beat the hell out of Aunt Mary. Considering he was a huge man and she was a small frame woman; it was a wonder he didn't kill her. Aunt Mary was so good to him and like a good country wife; she always had his meals on the table in a timely fashion. She was such a good cook and she made these awesome desserts. Her glasses would always slide down her nose and she would have to tilt her head upward to see you. I loved to study her face because it had these deep fine wrinkles around her mouth and the creases were filled with brown snuff juice. LMAO! I remember at one meal seeing her snuff drip down from her mouth into the green beans and I refused to eat them but never told her I saw it happen because I was afraid to hurt her feelings. It was only when she insisted that I eat her great green beans, that I screamed, "If I eat those beans Aunt Mary, I'm going to puke"! Aunt Mary just thought I was getting sick. If she only had known!

Living on the farm in those days, the houses had no heat or air conditioning. We would have to use the outhouse during the day and cold metal pots inside the house in our bedrooms for night potties. In the winter time you got out of bed to a cold house and it stayed that way until the cook stove in the kitchen got burning good so we could get dressed by it. We took baths in the kitchen in a large metal tub with hot water heated on the cook stove. In many ways farm living was good because I learned how to chase the cows in for the evening without getting trampled and in the morning helped to milk them. You see back in those days cows were milked by hand!

4

Butchering the Pigs & Chickens

I did not really want to know how farmers butchered pigs but I had no choice. Farm kids in those days grew up knowing all about the process and us three city slickers learned quickly that we would be treated no differently. Uncle George would head for the hog pen to shoot the hog between its eyes and hang it up on a teepee style structure made to hold the weight of the hog to let it bleed out and then he gutted it. When he got to the intestines the stink permeated the air and we disappeared quickly. Later on in the process I was taught how to slice big hunks of fat from the pig skin to make homemade lard for cooking.

It was Aunt Esters job to butcher the chickens. It seemed simple enough, yet messy and little scary looking. She grabbed the chicken and chopped their heads off but I have since heard variations such as wringing their heads off or hanging them upside down by their feet and puncturing them in the brain, letting them bleed to death. It didn't matter because it was terrifying to watch. The first time I saw this ritual of killing the chickens by chopping their heads off, I took off screaming because the chickens continue to run around with their heads off flinging blood everywhere. I just knew that damn chicken was going to get me. Aunt Ester just rolled laughing at me.

It was another laughing day for everyone as I was told to gather up wood chips from the chicken yard to be used to start the wood stove. You see, there was this crazy, very fast and mean rooster named Ollie that decided to attack me one day and after throwing the bucket of chips at him, Uncle George grabbed me up, screaming at me for being scared of a little ole rooster. He had no sympathy for this city girl! Needless to say, I stayed away from Ollie every chance I got!

5

The Outhouse and the Tractor

When we first moved in, we gave them plenty to laugh since we were city dwellers. where we had toilets that flushed and we bathed in a tub with hot running water coming from a faucet. The very day we moved in, my brother, Ken, was playing with his bat and ball.

He came running to the house excited because he hit the ball over the phone booth, until Aunt Ester explained what an outhouse was!! All of us kids thought it was the most disgusting smell when we were finally introduced to where we would be going to the bathroom. We were all given lanterns to carry to the outhouse at night. One night my little brother snuck off alone wanting to show he wasn't scared and that almost turned into a recovery effort! He accidently dropped the lantern down the hole and then proceeded to reach for it.

Uncle George heard him screaming and found him almost in the hole. Of course, it didn't end well at all after the whipping he got from Uncle George! You have to know that farm life for us little city slickers was all new and adventurous at the same time. I remember seeing my sister get up on the farm tractor and pretend she was driving.

However, she pulled the shifter just like she had seen the farm hand "Joe" do and the tractor started rolling down the hill. Needless to say, he was chasing it as fast as he could run to save her from hitting this huge boulder at the bottom of the hill. She hung on for dear life, but when she had stopped abruptly, Uncle George was standing there as well and jerked her off the tractor and beat her all the way back to the house. He beat her so hard that she wet her pants and this was probably the start of the many beatings we all got during the course of living on the farm.

There was a farm hand named "Joe" that we use to tease a lot because he was, to us, not a normal average adult, not knowing that he was a little mentally slower than most of his age. I made up a jingle singing *"Joe cut off his toe and hung it up to dry, all the girls began to laugh and Joe began to cry"*. He would get tickled at me singing it and use to give us kids Dentyne gum. Joe had a bad habit of chewing tobacco and taking the wad out of his mouth and putting it up on the fence post and come back later after his chores to put it back in his mouth. I got the bright idea to put chicken poop in the middle of it and when he came back, we watched as he put it in his mouth. Oh my God! I got the worse whipping I ever got from Uncle George too!

6

Devastating Experience

Uncle George was not the nice man everyone made him out to be. I still think about how he abused me as a child when he would get us up in the middle of the night to sit on those cold metal pot we used to go to the bathroom. It sat on the bedroom floor so we didn't have to go outside to the out-house. He would always get my brother and sister up first, put them back into their bed. Then he would get me up, and after putting me back in my bed, he would tell me to lay still and he would make me feel good. I didn't understand what was happening to me and I was really scared and would start to cry. He would take his belt off and tell me to be quiet and not to tell anyone or he would beat me with it. I was so afraid of him because it happened frequently and I never told Aunt Ester. She never was able to see signs of me having been abused because Uncle George was the only one allowed to bathe us children. I often wondered how she didn't know something was going on. To this day my mother went to her grave never knowing that he molested me as a young innocent child.

Things became more and more evident that living with Uncle George and Aunt Ester were not going to work out because Mom had fallen behind in paying them for our care and they were demanding her to come and get us and bring them the money she owed them. Leaving the farm was difficult because they refused to give mom our clothes because she told them she didn't have the money to pay them what she owed. Uncle George was a very threatening man. My sister, brother and I left the farm with only the clothes on our back and no coats to keep us warm on a very cold winter night. Not a good experience for three small innocent children to have to go through in the middle of the night.

7

Our Lives Turned Upside Down

Our lives turned upside down in so many ways and Mom was again in a situation that would soon lead to us children being placed in someone else's care. None of Mom's siblings were able to take us in to care for us for a long period of time so it was decided we would be better off in a stable environment where we would have better care, go to school and even attend church.

There was a family in Winchester, VA that was recommended to my mother that could help raise us. Arrangements were made and we soon were on our way. I believe this was sometime in the year of 1961 and we managed to stop by where our maternal grandmother lived in Winchester, VA. She lived on East Piccadilly Street on a very quiet, reserved street with a lot of older retired people. Grandma worked as a housekeeper and cooked meals for a man in return for a place to live. They were both in their 70's and seemed to get along fine. Grandma's first husband, whom she had two children by, had died in his 30's from pneumonia during the depression and she remarried and had five more children. Mom was the youngest and definitely her baby girl.

Grandma would cook and fill the table with food and pies when we came to visit. There would be both chocolate meringue and lemon meringue pies, and coconut custard pie, not to mention the jars of hard candies she had sitting around the house that we could eat whenever we wanted. As children, you can imagine, it was our favorite place to visit. Grandma was always worried about her baby daughter, and would often give her money she had saved from her social security check.

Mom finally told her that she would not be able to keep us because her job required her to work late into the nights as she had gotten a new job in Bailey's Crossroad, VA as a Manager of a local bar and grill called Admiral Grill. It was a hang- out for some of the country music singers in the Washington, D.C and Virginia area. She told Grandma we would be leaving after dinner and would be going to a nice family in Winchester at the foot of North Mountain. I remember seeing the tears in Grandma's eyes as she hugged and kissed us all goodbye. You see, Grandma was not able to take care of us at that time or I'm sure she would have. It was such a sad day for me, being the oldest, because I loved Grandma so much and really wanted to stay with her. I was her favorite of all her grandchildren even though she loved them all.

8

Ride to the New Farm

Our ride to the new farm was quiet and a little tense for Mom. Approaching the driveway, I could see the tears running down Mom's cheeks as she tried to wipe them away. We got a little excited as we saw a pond at the end of the driveway and Mom had told us there were other kids to play with. We too didn't want to be separated from Mom again, unfortunately we were too young to be given a choice.

The car stopped at the end of the driveway and Mom cut off the engine. A woman with long disheveled gray hair appeared in the doorway of the side porch of the old farm house but there were no other children in sight. We got out of the car and this woman greeted us and told us her name was Mrs. Anderson and to come into the house for a cold sweet ice tea. When we got into the kitchen there were other children sitting around an old wooden table eating pie. They were quietly eating their dessert. It was suggested at this time by Mrs. Anderson that we join the other children and have some dessert too. She also recommended that our mother not stay too long so we could get adjusted better the sooner she was gone. I guess she wanted us not to have anxiety separation in front of the other children. Needless to say, that didn't work. As soon as Mom got up from the table and gave us our hugs and kisses, we all three just started sobbing making it very hard for her to pull away. After what seemed like an eternity, she was able to let Mrs. Anderson take control and she took us in another room while Mom left through the kitchen door. I will never forget that moment and being the oldest, I just wanted to comfort my sister and brother. We were told at this time to call her Mrs. A and she then took us upstairs and showed us where we would sleep. Each of us were put in a separate room from each other right from the start. My sister and brother started screaming that they wanted to sleep with me because they were scared. Almost immediately the discipline came into play.

We soon learned after Mom left us there, that Mrs. Anderson would be a woman to fear and unbeknown to Mom, she had left us with horrible abusive people! It wasn't long before we knew that Mrs. A was a psycho bitch who abused the children she was entrusted with.

All three of us were abused to the point that we were scared to death to even come home from school. Many days there were whippings with a big huge black belt by Mr. Anderson. I remember returning home one day and Mrs. A had two of the youngest little foster girls, Sarah and

Tina upstairs in their bed twisting their little legs back towards their heads. There were blood curdling screams coming from that room. I just wanted to cry for these kids because they were so sweet. To keep them from being hurt any further I yelled for her to leave them alone! She turned and grabbed me demanding to know why I was up there and not downstairs doing homework. She started to pull me by my hair as she led me to the stairs and told me to go downstairs. I screamed for her to stop and to leave us alone. That probably was the worst thing I could do because it just infuriated her more. Fortunately, I heard Mr. Anderson come home and he called her to come downstairs. I ran to Sarah and Tina to hug them and I tried to make them feel better but they were so afraid and still trembling.

Living with the Anderson's was our worst nightmare of many we experienced through our young lives. We lived in fear wishing Mom would return to take us away from the horror we went through. I remember being one of the older children and constantly being made to clean, wash dishes, clothes and scrub floors. There were times I really believed I was Cinderella and anytime the wicked step-mother was about to lock me in a deep dark musty smelling basement. In the evenings when it came time for bed there was always turmoil and kids being whipped for dumb little things like not peeing in the potty fast enough to suit Ms. A, or not falling asleep quick enough to suit the old bitch!

Mr. and Mrs. Anderson's son, Freddie, age 16, seemed to like me. At age ten, I was one of the older girls in the house full of foster children. I had already started developing at an early age and he would reach under my shirt to touch my boobies. He liked to make me sit on his lap and he told me he wanted me to be his girlfriend. It would be our secret and he would give me a special gift for keeping a secret.

I was afraid of him. As much as I did not want to be around Mrs. A, when I saw Freddie coming I went looking for her or Diane, their older daughter. Diane was a few years older than me and I liked to hang around her. She was always fighting with Freddie so that made a perfect time to get away from him. I was so confused and scared of him that I would hide whenever he would come in the house. He always came looking for me and eventually would find me! I prayed for God to make him stop Freddie from all his horrible game playing with me but prayers were never answered. This is probably the reason when I attended church that it was hard for me to believe there was this wonderful God that we prayed too!

9

An Evil Woman

The Anderson's faithfully attended church every Sunday. It didn't help them a bit because they were such evil people to children and the biggest phonies to the outside world. I was made to go to a viewing of an old dead man that I didn't know. I guess it was one of Mrs. A's friends. I was upset being around these scary looking old people. We were in line to go into the funeral home and all these old people were hugging me. They smelt nasty to me and I guess it was because in those days they only took a bath once a week, usually on Saturday nights! As we approached this thing that I thought was a huge jewelry type box with the lid open, I could see someone was laying in it. Without any warning I was picked up by Mrs. A and made to touch this person and kiss them on the forehead. I was petrified and started screaming but that didn't stop her from making sure that I had felt this cold corpse. She whispered in my ear for me to shut up or she would put me in the coffin with him. I was so scared I shut the hell up because there was no way I wanted to lay beside that shriveled up old man! On the way home, she drove to this wooded area just a few miles from the house where there was a creek that crossed through it. She jerked me out of the car and took me to the creek that was partly froze over and told me to get into the frozen water. I was horrified and couldn't move so she shoved me in the freezing water and told me this was my punishment for screaming at the funeral home. I really don't know how long I was in the water but it seemed like forever to me. She finally jerked me out of the water and dragged me back to the car. She made me ride on the floor board of the back seat because she didn't want me to sit on her seats being all wet. I was shivering and sobbing all the way home.

When we arrived home, again she jerked my arm and dragged me in the house up the steps and proceeded to take off my wet clothes and called Mr. A upstairs. He too was a violent person and at her command he started beating me with a huge black belt all over my naked body. He always made Mrs. A take our clothes off before he would beat us.

I wasn't able to go to school for a couple weeks and Mrs. A told them I was sick with pneumonia! When I returned to school, I was so withdrawn from all my friends and even my teacher. I knew if I told her what really had happened to me, I would fear for my life. Mr. Anderson himself was a man to be scared of when he took me in the room behind the kitchen, which they called a pantry, and would just glare at me up and down before he would pull my pants down and whip me for a stupid thing like not drying the glasses to a sparkling shine after washing. All of us were so fearful of even breathing a word to an outsider about anything that was happening to us in their home. If only my teacher had seen the bruises for herself and made an attempt on her own to find out, just maybe we could have been saved from these horrible people.

My brother, Ken, was only six years old and in the first grade when we lived with the Anderson's. There was only one other boy and that was Freddie. He was always taking my brother for bicycle rides, putting him on the handle bars while he rode down the road to the Barber to get their hair cut. He seemed happy to be spending time with Freddie and was always saying he didn't like to be in the house without him. I guess he kind of looked at Freddie as being his older brother.

One day after they came back from getting their haircuts, my brother sat down at the dinner table and saw corn on his plate. He hated corn and told Mrs. A he didn't want to eat it but she made him take a bite at which time he spit it out on his plate. Mrs. A immediately grabbed him up from the dinner table, as we all looked in horror, as she dragged him, along with his plate into the pantry and closed the door. We could hear him crying and begging, but later he told us she was shoving the corn in his mouth and he got sick and spit it all over the floor. She shoved him down on his knees and told him to eat the food off the floor like a dog and he apparently refused. It was then we heard him screaming as he was being whipped so hard, he couldn't sit down for a week.

Weeks later we were all outside playing and we saw the cow get through the fence. We all ran and hid under the picnic table as we saw Mrs A come out of the house screaming at us to find out who let the cow out. My little brother got blamed, even though the cow got out on its own, and he got the beating. He hated Mrs. A and would come crying to me that he wanted Mom to come and get us.

My brother, even as young as he was, started saving his lunch money because he thought if he made enough money for Mom, she would come and take us home away from this mean ole' woman.

He came home from school one day and he was immediately called to the front room by Mrs. A and in her hand was his little satchel of money that he kept hidden in his dresser drawer. He was forced to tell the truth about why he was hiding his lunch money and was told that if our mother had wanted us to live with her and loved him, she wouldn't have bought him there to live. Mr. A took off his black belt and told him to lean across the foot stool, at which time he pulled his pants down and gave him a whipping to remember. Later on, they made my brother spend all the money on a new pair of shoes.

Each night we ate our dinner at a big wooden table in the Allison's kitchen. Two of the foster children, Sarah and Tina, sat on the backside bench of the table and they always had a terrified look on their face. Every night Mrs. A would warn them not to piddle with their food. She would give this warning three times and then she would snatch them up from their seats and drag them to the pantry that was right off the kitchen and beat the hell out of them! She showed them no mercy. It was no wonder that every night at dinner time their little hands would shake. I was scared to death she would start on us next because several times we got the warning of, "stop piddling with your food"!

One snowy morning all the kids were playing outside, my sister picked up a snowball and threw it hitting Sarah in the back but she was just playing and not trying to be mean. All of a sudden she threw up and started crying. Mrs. A came running and asked what happened.

Everyone told her my sister threw a snowball at Sarah and hit her in the back. Mrs. A looked at her telling her at four o'clock that day she was going to give her a whooping. She waited all day and thought for sure she forgot because she never said another word about it through the day.

I was wrong! At four o'clock on the dot she called my sister to come to the foyer. I was sick to my stomach because I saw the whippings Sarah and Tina got. She grabbed her, stripped off her clothing and took a paddle to her butt. It seemed like she would never stop hitting her.

It was dinner time and my sister was not feeling well. Mrs. A called for us to come to dinner. My sister was not hungry and I knew if she didn't eat, she would get beat. She tried not to be obvious picking at her food but she still spotted her piddling and gave the warning. She quickly ate the remaining food. After dinner she told my sister, brother and I that our mom was coming the next day for a visit. Afterwards Mrs. A grabbed my sister and warned her to stay away from our mother when she came and not to get in her lap like usual. She also warned her about telling my mother that she loved her. These were warnings that we all took very seriously because we knew what she was capable of and we were terrified of this crazy woman. We knew we had to be able to talk to mom if we were ever to get out of this place.

The next day my sister was still sick and feeling much worse. The glands in her neck hurt so bad making it very difficult to eat or even talk and she was so scared. Mom was going to join us for lunch and I knew my sister would not be able to eat. When mom arrived, she did as Mrs. A had ordered her to do. She sat on the backside of the table on the bench with the other little girls and stayed quiet. Mom took a seat at the table and Mrs. A was talking to her like she was her best friend. My sister could not eat because she was just too sick.

She got the warning to stop piddling but it did not matter. There was a pause, and mom realized she had not run over to give her a hug. I heard Mom ask if she was sick but she could not answer. The tears started to stream down my sister's cheeks and I could see the panic in her face because she was so afraid of Mrs. A. Mom asked me to come over to her and I could tell my sister didn't know what to do. Mom must have picked up on something because she insisted for my sister to come to her. She got up to walk over to her hoping Mrs. A would not stop her. She jumped into mom's lap and held on to her for dear life soaking her with tears. Mom felt her head and told Mrs. A that she was burning up with fever and questioned why Mrs. A had not taken her to the doctor because my sister's glands were very much enlarged. Mom was very upset with Mrs. A and told her to get our things together that she was taking us with her.

Such a feeling of relief came over me and I knew once out of this sick woman's house we would be able to share with mom all that happened but for some reason we were so glad to be with her we didn't say a word. I felt safe once again! My brother and I didn't waste any time getting upstairs to pack our belongings, while my sister stayed in Mom's lap.

As we were leaving the house, Mrs. A told mom that she could bring us back anytime she was ready. This was just a front to make her look good in our mother's eyes, but our mom knew that her Mrs. A's caregiving was not up to par and she may have to make other arrangements one more time for us!

Mom immediately took my sister to the doctor. At first, they thought it was the mumps but then Mom told them it couldn't be because she already had them. The doctor told mom it was a very serious infection that required hospitalization. They gave my sister shots around the clock and wrapped hot water bottles around her neck for the enlarged glands. They did not know what caused it but they suspected contaminated milk. Today, I can't help but wonder if Mrs. A tried to poison her!

We never found out what Mom did about Mrs. A's care after she finally found out only the way were treated in that foster home. I suspect that she may have turned them in to the Social Services but we were never returned to them.

More than fifty years later, after we all had raised our own families, my sister, brother and I got together for a trip down memory lane and rekindled the bond as brother and sisters. The memories of living with the Anderson's, as we discussed the abuse, it was evident that my brother experienced more trauma than we thought. Seems that he paid dearly for not sitting still in church. I remember the day he came home holding his hand and crying loudly as she pushed him through the door. She had squeezed his fingers so badly in church. As he cried out in pain. Of course, to other church members in those days, it appeared to be a mild form of disciplinary action, but she had broken two of his fingers right there in church.

Two days after the incident in church, my brother had to be taken to the doctor because he could not even hold a pencil for school and his fingers were so swollen and bruised. She told the doctor that he injured his fingers while playing softball, trying to catch a flyball without his glove on. She was a very convincing liar to all who knew her and we did not dare to challenge her explanations to others. I remember while he was telling us his story, that my brother did get very quiet during the rest of our stay with the Anderson's. He didn't talk to anyone in school just like me after my incident with Mrs. A and he didn't like to go outside to play as well.

You can bet that out of the three of us, my brother hated the Anderson's the most as he continues to tell us that in his twenty's he returned to the Anderson home with a friend who had to go there on business.

First, he didn't realize where he was going but after he arrived, he knew exactly where he was and who the people were. He said he had fun messing with them and watching how uncomfortable he was making them as he explained to his buddy that the house had changed with all the additions and the big picture window had been moved over. He kept his conversation between him and his buddy low keyed, but was talking loud enough for the Anderson's to hear. He actually caught the two of them out of the corner of his eyes looking at him possibly realizing who he may be. He didn't elaborate too much with his buddy because his buddy was doing business with them, explaining to us that he was sure from their reaction that they may not have slept very well that night. After all, my brother was very revengeful and no one knew what he may be capable of doing.

After our first get together we decided to meet up on the following Saturday to take a road trip out to Winchester, VA to do a little investigating ourselves. Our brother was late and he didn't seem to be in a good mood when he arrived. My sister asked if he didn't get enough sleep the night before and he said he wasn't feeling well and wasn't hungry. He actually told us he only showed up to give us directions to the Andersons's and a few specifics he had found out. we were also excited to get started that we didn't even notice that Ken seemed to be preoccupied. Needless to say, we cancelled our trip and decided to see what was going on in Ken's world. What was on Ken's mind was something we would soon find out and never forget!

11

The Devils Revenge

In Ken's mind he could never get over the abuse we suffered living with the Anderson's It was as if he were possessed by the Devil to do something awful about it since that day he returned to their house with a friend who was doing some remodeling. Both of the Andersons appeared to be threatened by his sudden appearance and the fact he recognized some not forgotten features of their home when he went with his friend that day.

He glared at Mrs. A so hard that it was very unnerving to her. He knew then she was scared and he feverishly began to plot his devilish revenge.

Months later Ken returned to the Andersons's home unbeknown to his sisters. Approaching the driveway in broad daylight, he wasn't sure what he would encounter that day but after watching the house for several hours he somehow knew that Mrs. A was alone. He decided to move into action with his plan. Parking his vehicle about three hundred feet from the house near the pond between an over growth of trees, he moved forward he could see Mrs. A through the living room picture window and watched her get into her lazy boy chair where she often would nap during the day when no one was around. He slowly crept up to the front door, opened the unlocked screen door, thinking the whole time how stupid she was in this day and time for leaving her door unlocked! He could hear her blood curdling snoring, with its gurgling and squawking pauses like the sound the Devil makes when he is about to pound on human flesh!

Not hesitating any longer, he lunged for the chair, grabbing her around the neck and pulling her out of the chair. He could see the fear of God in her eyes as he pointed the 357 Magnum at her. He started yelling, "You are going to pay for what you've done to me and my sisters. "Yes, remember me, I'm the one whose fingers you broke in church Bitch!" He dragged her out of the house by her hair, down through the field to the car, all the time telling her what pay backs she was about to face for abusing us. She begged him not to shoot her and he replied" Don't worry, that's not good enough for you! I've got better plans for your departure from this world and just know that the Devil has you by the hand now and you are going down!" She pleaded with him more, talking about her God and how he would forgive him for his sins. This only made Ken more aggressive with her and he tied her hands behind her back with the same belt he took from the house that he was abusively beat with as a child. He shoved her into the car and drove her a short distance further from the house to the same creek where years ago she had taken our sister and tortured her for screaming and making a scene in the funeral home because Mrs. A made her touch and kiss a dead body!

He stopped the car and yanked her from the seat. It was in the dead of winter and the creek was just as icy as the day she made our sister strip off her clothes and get into the icy water. History was about to repeat itself, only it would be her this time who experienced what a young child went through that day years ago! He untied her hands and made her strip down and then forced her into the water. He made her stay there until the exposure of the cold icy water caused her to pass out but he knew she was still alive. He then dragged her by her arms out of the water and threw her limp less body into the trunk of the car. He drove on further into the woods where he previously dug a grave. Inside of this grave was a coffin he had stolen the night before from a local funeral home. Opening the trunk, he could see she was shivering and begging for mercy. With the Sledge hammer he retrieved from the backseat of the car, he grabbed her hand and broke two of her fingers! Removing her from the trunk he was screaming at her "You will reach your final destination soon and suffer the agonies of hell getting there, suffocating into purgatory!" and also reminding her how she tried to slowly poison our little sister that put her in the hospital near death and leaving her scarred for life from the abusive beatings. "Yes, you evil bitch, it's time for you to die!" He pushed her screaming and begging once more for her life down into the coffin. Watching the horrid look on her face as he slowly closed the coffin and telling her she would never again be able to hurt and cause pain to another child! Hurryingly he covered her grave with branches of pine trees, setting it on fire and sending her burning into hell!

Ken left that day, never to return, only to send my sister and I a letter telling us what he had done and no matter what may happen to him, he loved us. He wanted us to know the very details of her death and that he got revenge for all us! To this day Ken has never been captured and brought to trial for the murder of Mrs. Anderson!

12

Closure

For these three children who fell victim to so much turmoil and abuse growing up, they never seem to find closure until they grow up, get married and have families of their own.

Even then their lives for happy marriages grow apart and divorce is inevitable. It certainly does not end here as you will find that their struggles as children have now grown up with them in their adult lives and their stories are amazingly touching, to say the least, as they try very hard to raise and protect their own children from falling victim to such horrible memories!